FROM MONKEY to MONK

74 Poems

By C.L. Smith

From Monkey to Monk
Author: C. L. Smith:

Cover Design
Artist: C.L. Smith

Copyright 2015, 2016

ISBN 978-0-9792530-3-4

Published January 24, 2016

**Dedication
to**

**Robin & Alex
two magnificent people
in my life**

Preface

I do not believe that being born in America makes you an American. Traipsing across the border doesn't make you an American any more than writing poems will make you a poet. Being American is not a political, religious, capitalistic or racial endeavor. The founders of America were individuals working together to form a more perfect union of people than history has known: a country by the people and for the people. As Americans, we are committed to being responsible citizens.

It is our union that enables justice, and domestic tranquility. It is our union that provides the blessing of liberty. Harmony and freedom is our prosperity as is health our wealth. Our treasures are our families and friends, to love and to be loved. We must be united not in our pursuit but in our desire to excel, we are not pirates and thieves, are we?

As Homo sapiens we have endured eons of blind progressions of mythic and genetic posturing, our instincts have been honed to an intelligent awareness. It doesn't matter whether we have faith in what we don't know or believe in what we do know, to survive we are now tasked to proceed in a civilized manner. We must not let our hunger distract us from our direction.

Our patriotism now entails a journey of global relationships, of global responsibilities; a strategy of united nations. As we ingest the growing database of fresh information, Science and Art aspire to new depths. Look around, talent and goodwill flourish everywhere. New modes of collaboration expand our capacity to advance our conditions.

The success of our determination thrives not on sacrifice but on goodwill, not on innovation but on respecting our intricacies.

We are now so focused and detailed in our diligence that even our physics has evolved from the study of fossils to a quantum curiosity about our nature, venturing as far as the notion of questioning as to whether we actually exist.

I have written and present these poems in case we do.

if the pen
is mightier
than the sword
why is there
a waiting period
to buy guns
but not one
to buy pencils

raindrops do not fall, they jump
without trepidation or parachute
they leap out into the immense sky
plummeting ever so wildly downward
racing faster and faster descending
seconds per second, pressing their
round moist bodies forward
zooming closer and closer
toward the proximity of landscape

splat! mission accomplished

with an abrupt kamikaze plunk
they collide with all creatures
and creation alike
splattering across mountains,
forests, fields and gardens,
plunging into the depths of oceans,
lakes and streams, crashing onto
roofs and windows, picnics and parades

undeterred by umbrellas
the raindrops wait patiently
for the warm sunshine
to pull them back up again
lifting them back onto the clouds

we are not raindrops
but they are inside us

the
narrow
burden
of
the
cow
is
not
to
feel
flies
and
give
milk
but
to
kiss
grass
and
swallow
life

have a nice day
have a nice day
have a nice day

yeah, yeah
like I'm supposed to
pick one off the shelf
and take it in paper or plastic

maybe when I'm traveling
down the street and see
an ambulance pulled over
I'll run over and say
here, have a nice day

or maybe give it
to some wide eyed
sockless dude
sifting through the dumpster

or how about that Vet
home from doing his duty
missing a leg and three buddies
here, have a nice day

nah, I think I'll just go home
and play my harmonica awhile
wait until they go on sale

while counting
the dangers of
standing still

while this beautiful fog
which no dream need fix
parades along the city's
frail spine

while orbiting fires
define sky

another name
for rose
escapes from
your skin tight laughter

stay in the moment

will you teach me how master

yes, in a moment

dictating parks
to pigeons

Newton explained
the apple
but he didn't
explain the tree

Albert explained
the relatives
but neither
you or me

the hot lines
all have numbers
you can call for free
anytime you'd like
to acquire their
catechism tea

preachers are just peaches
masquerading under fuzz
life defies its gravities
by falling into love

frost on the pumpkins
walls tumbling down
forget spreading wings
just use less ground

stop your fencing
lay down your sabers
it's good dancing
that makes good neighbors

love is not an asking
a moment or a proof
a sunlight made for basking
nor household under roof

love is not a flower
a season or a face
it isn't even giving
or putting into place

and more it isn't shadow
or energy's intention
a flowing stream
or sugar cream
nor secret self correction

love is not a rose
a practice or a way
a circle without gender
or price you needn't pay

love is not a certain kiss
it's not a master code
it's not the same as like a lot
or pi in Allah mode

and though our future be
all that never was
it doesn't matter what love is
as matters what love does

I say his death was no accident
(though sudden and too soon)
nor was it malignant tumors
that brought him to his doom

neither was it clogged arteries
his heart and lungs were fine
not a virus or infection
nor excess food and wine

no his death was all related
to the nature of his crime
I believe he died as just reward
for killing too much time

like
a drizzling
rain
murdering
soil
into
mud
we make
slaves
out of things
rather than
master
ourselves
emancipating
speech
so that
money
can
speak

got clowns
in the kitchen
crack'n up
the cornflakes
got jokers
in the deck
stack'n up
the puncakes

for a journey of
a thousand smiles
or eggs in search
of bacon
there is no path
to follow
only steps
to be taken

yes
your underwear
but mostly
your everywhere
sets myself on fire
like luck tumbling thru dice
or alerted birds
escaping ritual sky

the persuasion of
your shoeless imagination
construes an absolute chemistry
of virtue and exhilaration

not water into wine
blood into life

used to be a day
when ya could
go out back
and grap a squirrel
squinch a fish
or tap a few eggs

nows ya gots to
jingle gold
to snack a spread
or dunk your soul
in a lousy swill of fudge

ya gots to don a suit
spiff your shoes and walk
the straight and narrow

ya gots to have a license
for that ego

does ya thinks maybe
someday they's gonna concoct
plastic burgers to chomp
that will schwink us with
wrinkle free skin
and shatter proof bones
dianetically calibrated
to April

ya just gots to eat
more sparkplugs

sometimes
I imagine trees
after their leaves have fallen,
without their branches

a hillside of trees
all without leaves
and without branches
not trees that sway and rustle
moodily with every breeze
I imagine tall trees
serenely stretching
embracing afternoon sky

sometimes
I imagine climbing one
scaling limb
by invisible limb
up its trail of spiraling
invitations to ascend
then
perched quietly
overlooking the hillside
I watch for birds who
sometimes
fly by
without wings

great minds
think alike

what
is known
is only
enough
to ask
more
questions
but
if love
opens
cages
why seek
answers

wisdom
is concise
ignorance

shallow minds
think alike

Picasso
Dali
& Klee
mastered
titanium
cadmium
and zinc

)surreally
rendering(

feelings
as
thoughts
we feel
&
thoughts
as
feelings
we think

I didn't become

a one mean son of a bitch

reading about it

thirsting
for simple moisture

the last rose
lay in its bed dying
its frail petals
unable to open,
its once cavalier thorns
mere useless hooks,
its leaves curled
and withering

my piano is ill too

evading
discouragement
I put on my shoes
walk to the Silver Spoon
and have a cheddar omelet
while I read the Times

I circle the ad for
Master Piano Technician

the waitress
doesn't expect a 30% tip
but I do anyway

a bowl of buttons
won't feed anyone
so we play checkers
on dad's flannel shirt
we do double
and even triple jumps
yet no one ever gets hurt

we play to be kings
so we can move backwards
(kings are bigger in size)
we never cheat
when the other isn't looking
the buttons are checkers with eyes

while
mr & mrs god
(resting on various elbows)
muse over rash judgments
made to poison ivy,
winter drifts
into the evening sky

snowflakes crystalize
out of the brute darkness
escorting the moon's borrowed
argument of sunlight
down to the brittle divinity
of ice shackled trees
emancipating
acorns
from
apostrophe
posture

giving
snowballs
a chance in hell

now that I've cried
upon the moon's shoulder
stood in the darkness
grown a bit older

now that I've watched
the rain slowly stream by
without knowing how long
and without asking why

now that I've drifted
with snow to my knees
blown with the wind
like leaves from their trees

now that I've danced
without music or song
heard the birds sing
without singing along

and even now
though your kiss
is no longer my wine
I can still feel
your warm lips
upon mine

seldom do
scarecrows
consider corn
yet some
monkeys escape
from the circus
to join the zoo
but there is no
organ grinder
so
they join the army
but there are no
peanuts
so they charter planes
into the jungle
but there are no
clowns
so they go back
to the circus
and wait for
bananas
to be
invented

the incidence
of birth
a whimper
a bang
the short cuts
of thorns
from which
roses sprang

the moons
of circumstance
their rise
their fall
the short cuts
of meaning
parading
recall

through life
flows love
the short cuts
of trying
there is
no death
only dying

I wish I could provide you
with kindness and tenderness
as does a fragile rose

I wish I could provide harmony
and peace, a fullness of breath
the clarity of sunlight etching
morning upon the horizon

I wish I were the moonlight
or the un-intruding brilliance
of distant stars segmenting darkness

I wish I were the serene height
of snowcapped mountains
invoking patience into blue sky

I wish I were a purling stream
you could dangle summer feet in
cooling your heels
from the jungle of purpose

I wish I were a windmill of flowers
the rustle of tumbling autumn leaves
the laughter of children
from the schoolyard
the comfort of a rocking chair
on the back porch

perhaps I should just wish
to hold your hand awhile longer
as I drink tomorrow
from the fountain of your smile

from monkey to monk
the thinkers all thunk
that apples are in the eye

half wittedly devoted
they strayed and misquoted
the promise of pie in the sky

with beddings of bunk
wet dreams were drunk
and wishing wells ran dry

their scruples eroded
populations exploded
now big fish are eating small fry

lovabetical
loverious
lovindular
lovogical
lovulant

lovantific
loverial
lovitamins
lovopular
lovuntarily

lovamatic
loversatile
lovitarian
lovotical
lovuality

Tex echo station
pump 9 blaring Kansas
like a Saturday night jukebox

(if all we are is dust in the wind
who's playing the violin)

asking for directions with a smile
echoing where is the road
echoing lost
echoing a smile
on the lost road echoing
where is the road
which way is lost
echoing a smile out loud
is that way
the way

only for the moment
I echo, with a dusty smile
a lost smile

we can be all there is
wind, sand and star
but before we can change
we must become what we are

there may be roads less traveled
and horizons yet uncharted
but the time to be or not to be is now
the future has already started

leaning against sunset
I let poems write
themselves

I let poetry slice
the moon into inspiration
stars into glimmers of hope
the relentless ocean into dreams

I let poetry rhyme
death with breath
dismay with hooray
strategy with tragedy
and never with forever

I let poetry extol
alligators for their luggage
floss deadwood
from sharp toothed clocks
and weave threads
for life to hang on to

then as dawn breaks
courageously
I let the world turn
all by itself
while I tame
the wild flowers

it is logical

to put a door in a wall

but not a salad

"What is love?"
Lady Jane asked
John Thomas replied by
putting flowers in her hair
D. H. stood up
and clapped
Plato fell asleep
in his not-so-easy chair

wasn't born yesterday
maybe tomorrow

love makes us equal
when love is true
because love is the heart
with the beautiful view

love takes the time
to forgive and to care
love gives us the courage
to trust and to share

love is the inspiration
for the good that we do
because love is the heart
with the beautiful view

at the edge of town
is my favorite sky
to meet my favorite friends

one loyal moon
and a billion stars
Pegasus
Cassiopeia
Aquarius
Orion
ancient graffiti
from cave dwellers
gone wild

we too are
constellations
orbiting
the darkness
connecting dem
head bones
to neck bones
to shoulder bones
to spine bones

hoping to get our
heads on straight
we share a potion
of cannabis outside the cave

they say
there is a devil
in a place
called hell
who will burn
your soul forever
for not living
life so well

but perhaps
the only demon
is the thought
inside your head
that says the life
that is within you
is worth more
when you are dead

one day
when nothing else matters
you will leave the back door open
all the birds will fly in
all the animals and critters
will shuffle in and fill up the whole place
it will become too crowded to move
too noisy to sleep
but it won't matter because
you will die tomorrow
having forgotten to take
your vitamins for the last 32 years

unshaken by
sizemologists'
failure to
detect
the Rumba
of starlight
or Velocity
of time
the sweet Jazz
of your kiss
incites
my Heart
to dance with
the moons
of Jupiter
into a new
geography
of Foxtrot

starlight
evaporates

no dogs are barking

a baby faced moon
slumbers amid a nursery
of unkempt clouds

we embrace

ancient vocabularies
of Old Man River
stream through me
from the voice of
your nearness
as we journey
into kiss

right in
the middle
of the oval
universe

I did not see death
standing at the corner
whittling a bar of soap
shaping it into a gun
blackening it with soot
sticking it into my back
shooting into my
surprised spine
bursting my bubble

he looked like
an ordinary guy
wearing an ordinary hat
minding his own bubble

a bird
in the hand
is worth two
in the bush
unless
the bush
is at hand

in cases
like that
use the factor
of cat
inversely
with the claw
of demand

laughter's tears travel

intricately down your cheek

and water my heart

so many
broken dreams
like shattered glass

I tip toe around
the hurting edges
arranging seeds
for next year's almanac

systematically unjust
I restrict favors
to ward off loneliness
like a tincture
of perpetual
agreement
between
sackcloth
and
plowing
fields
with my
bare teeth

you called the police
when you saw a hillside of cows
because you saw their picture
on a milk carton
yet there are children missing

how crazy is that
stealing children
how pathetic
how does such a loser
how does such a lost soul exist
how angry
how outraged we should be
we need to shackle
these scum to the ground
and let the cows dribble their dung
onto these coward's heads
let them taste the putrid flatulence
of their own behavior
leave them to starve
unnourished by any sense of tolerance
release packs of hungry wolves
to shred their useless bones
their sharp angry teeth ripping apart
the slightest thought of forgiveness

as the sun set peacefully over the hillside
I tossed the carton into the recycle bin
yet there are children missing

will you
be sleeping
here tonight
or just waiting
by the window
for the light

(love does not
struggle to survive
but to be the fittest)

all your choices
may have voices
and
all your reasons
rhyme
but love
will only keep
your dreams awake,
not from under
the metric hooves
of marching
time

love is for lovers
love is why
love is for keeping
love passes by

love is for lovely
for living
and free
love answers
love asks
love is to be

love is for eating
for drinking
and touch
love is enough
love is too much

love can whisper
love can shout
love can know
love can doubt

when love is lived
love will show
when love is loved
love will grow

I am not as immortal
as I used to be
so
when death comes
I will not be sitting
on the patio
beneath the cool umbrella
near the pin striped piano player
sipping spritzers
snacking caviar Chopin

when death comes
I will be wearing
thick suspenders
a half buttoned shirt
and scuffed kick'n boots
pack'n a slick blade

when death comes
I'll slash off his legs
bust bottles and chairs
over his mug faced skull
gash out his eyes
and ridicule his manners

when you see him
you can tell him
I said so

give me your eyes
if seeing is believing
I will show you how
a kiss can make
beautiful babies
(each child
born of you
gives love
more hearts)
I have seen
the children
playing in the park
laughing, splashing
spiraling down the
water slide
asking to be born

maybe it weren't no apple
maybe it were a banana, the kid mocked the old man

do you think god made man on a small budget
of monkeys, he said squinting at the kid

do you think god can chew gum and create the world
at the same time, he quipped winking at the old man

maybe god made the world to just look like
it evolved, he rebutted, scoffing the kid

and I suppose god made the sky just big enough
so that birds can fly, he shot back at the old man

time is more precise than sand
he shouted tossing the hourglass at the kid
it smashed explosively against the wall behind him

now don't be dancing on the table
you'll get soup on your shoes, the kid spouted spryly
ducking the trajectory of the hourglass

they darted towards each other
bound for violent turmoil
when divertingly the game was back on
the commercial over, they retreated

the old man plumped back into his chair and
crushed a hand full of crackers over his chowder

how about double or nothing, the kid parleyed

without
milk
who
can be
a mother

perhaps the sky
whistles clouds
to disperse hue
to perennials
crazy
about
chlorophyll

I whistle
emptying
myself
knowing
you will
fill me
again

she
wearing
apple of
ignorance
perfume

he
talking
about
selling
self-folding
maps

stirring
the alphabet
for the last
word
they
rain
dance
into
capital
Love
negotiating
a backseat
to make
a little
Yes

Sarah wants a goodnight kiss
Martin wants a drink of water
Tina likes the light on
Lou the door left open

Peter wants a story read
Tammy just a lullaby
Toby needs an extra pillow
Karla her blue blanket

Sidney snugs his teddy bear
Glenda keeps her socks on
Jean whispers a private prayer
Roslyn writes into her journal

such are the delicate
instruments of dreams
the dark night prescribes

the dark night
which with a single moon
teaches all the wolves to howl

truth is a door
that never closes

love is a door
that always opens

beware the door
to door salesman

I am a fool
stumbling
through
moonlight
I could prove it
instead
you pull me
to your side
to hold you
as if I am strong
and brave
protecting you
from things
hiding in the dark
just waiting

I let you believe
I am strong
and brave
I let you look
into my eyes
to see
because I believe too
I am no longer
hiding in the dark
just waiting

so what if
paradigms do
keep shifting
and tables
always turn
why is enough
is enough
so hard to learn

is there justice
or just us

fingers finger
twirling twine
catting cradles
is just fine
for the game
is not to prove
but to make the
small balls move

to move beyond
the weight of fate
takes more than love
takes hating hate

I saw god the other day
standing on the corner
of Second & Vine
a bus stopped, he got on, I followed
he got off at St. Thomas' church
and went in

towering stained glass figures
haloed in piety looked on as
he solemnly bowed and lit a candle
at the shrine of the Holy Family

he then broke off one
of the enshrining flowers from
its stem and poked the stalk
into the basin of holy water
and sipped a drink through it

nobly pressing souvenir kisses
into the cheering silence
he patted his lips dry
and returned to the bus

I ran to him fervently
pleading for an answer
'Why do chickens cross the road?'

(prudently) he retorted
'To catch the bus.'
he then sputtered away
in a cloud of industrial smoke,

that was about six fifteen

delicate
balance

stone & stick
thin & thick
slow & quick
treat & trick
tock & tick

what
the
world
needs
now
is
more
old
people
who
aren't
always
getting
sick & sick

I kiss your roses

because the garden is full

of tender nipples

unday

blue ribbons
achieve their
gossip
with
professional
maidens
conversant
in 20 different
silences

a gazillion
sheep
obey their
fences
and come
to rest

white mind
drizzles
relevance
into
fresh
puddles
of razor sharp
love

no need
to manage
leftovers

new love
consumes
roses
by
the
dozen

cravings
for what
disapperson
into kiss
as love
unwhos
each

the rain
does not
merely
fall
it arrives
precisely
on time

each breath I take expels
a giant ghost
the whole world must be fricken zero

clouds shivering with snow
hover somberly in the winter grey sky
the wind's chill cuts into my flesh
like skates slicing across ice

my car is smothered in snow
its windshield glazed in ice
my ears pierced with frost
my fingers fricken icicles
and my feet a numb slush
in a knee deep drift

I should probably
buy a warmer coat
hooded and thermal lined
and some new gloves
instead
I will get some hot chocolate
and a sled for the fricken kids

the cost
of free will
is not charity
tis not giving
one iota
I ain't going to hell
I'm holdin' out
for scotch and soda

the cost
of free will
is not self-control
or fending off attackers
I ain't going to heaven
I'm holding out
for cheese and crackers

what we see
is what we get
like eating and drinking
there is no consciousness
just thinking
about thinking

you worm my heart
yes
you worm me for no reason
and without my deserving

you worm my troubled mind
as if you knew my every thought

I wake up in the middle of night
having dreamt of your worming smile
and the way it makes me feel

when I am cold
alone and it is dark
I imagine the world full
of worm people like you

did I say worm
I meant warm

you warm my heart
yes

the shuffling ends
i place my signature onto the dots
You Have Been Granted
Temporary Courage

thank you madamsir
But, You Must Love
Or It Will Be Repossessed

and i will become
a mumbling fearful salesman
Yes And Forced To Fornicate
With Drunken Sailors

will i make friends
You Do Not Make Friends
You Can Only Be A Friend

can i stop the war
Forgiving Is Your Sword

it's a two edged sword
No Grasshopper
It Has Four Edges Like The Others

i'll be a hero
You're Just A Big Baby

grandmother passed away last night
leaving her lavender robe draped
over her walker at the end of the bed
she passed through the hallway
lined with pictures
of proud soldiers wearing medals
and of smiling newlyweds,
pictures of the twins in identical suits
one of me in cap and gown at graduation
and a black and white of grandma
herself in pigtails on a tractor

she passed through the kitchen
around the dinette set and on by
the ornate sugar bowl
I gave her one Christmas
she passed around the tattered stacks
of indispensable Gazettes
on out through the back porch

she passed by the marigolds
the chrysanthemums
the black faced pansies
and the violets,
she passed through the maples
and the tall oak by the street
on up to the moon
out into the stars

grandmother passed away last night
she didn't stop to say goodbye

some silences
are louder than others
what the heart sings
may not always find lips

in your kiss
a thousand stars
champion darkness
to infuse hope
into my vague soul

you touch me
as if I exist

it's been a long time

since I have thought of stealing

a watermelon

we made love beneath the flag
it waved freely high above us

after the fighter jets
stopped blasting bombs
after the dust of pummeled buildings
and crumbling glass stopped falling
after the blaring sirens were silent
and the scorn of raging bullets had ceased,
while rogue fires still rummaged
through the rubble

we made love beneath the flag
just before we bled to death

one hand clasping her mirror
she applied another smudge of
cherry orchard gloss onto her open mouth
I want poetry I can feel
poetry that touches me
poetry I can FeeeL she exclaimed
slamming the mirror down

without whiskey
I tackled her to the floor
ripped her blouse open
stabbed her with mutilated soldiers
scorched her with a wild tragic fire
and tormented her with shoeless children
playing in the street,
then verse by verse
I caressed her with moonlight
shimmering across a summer lake
reflecting the sway of tall palm trees
her chest rose with a sigh of relief
as a freckle faced kid
and his cat were rescued from
a burning rooftop in my final poem,
clasping my hand
she settled peacefully into sleep
her plum lips punctuating her repose

I wrote some new buttons
back onto her blouse
then resumed searching
the neighborhood for my lost cat

I do not intend
slicing you into memory
meshing fragments
to comparison
cataloging expressions
estimating joy
footnoting masquerades

if I do try to peek
beneath your mask
it will not be for
truth or beauty
but to see if perhaps
I might be
under there too

dyslexic vegan

abstaining from diary

loses track of thyme

we are a good country
for allowing our citizens
to possess guns
we will be a great people
when we don't need them

birds flying to the sound
of a distant drum
not knowing where their next worm
is coming from
flying high in the sky
searching the ground
is that my dream I have found

I just want to cry
in your arms, mamma
feel your certainty
all my sorrows and sadness
my troubles and madness
disappear when you're with me

they keep killing
for diamonds, oil and gold
the days keep getting shorter
the nights are cold

soldiers fighting
trained to take it on the chin
soldiers dying
whose shoes are they walking in
sending drones to combat zones
make us safe and sound
tell me mamma,
is that my dream I have found

yes, we all have our freedoms
but the freedoms are not free
I just want to cry
in your arms, mamma
feel your certainty

ain't no use in howling at the moon, babe
ain't no use in looking to the sky
ain't no use in calling out my name, babe
if you can do it, you'll do it when you try
ain't no use in tapping at the window
ain't no use in knocking on the door
ain't no use in holding out your hand, babe
you've got it all, there isn't any more

feathers may be falling all around you
to shadow on the things that you know
but a heart of gold is always open
ready and willing to grow
Jesus was a bum rap on a high wire
crossed up by the fishes that he schooled
Shiva placed his bets on the wild fire
and danced away the evening like a fool
the Yellow Rose of Texas she done good, babe
untying all them ribbons from their trees
but the bullets she used were real, babe
ain't no one just shooting the breeze

well, I've never thought that I would die, babe
though there were times I couldn't take it any more
we can always be less than we are, babe
but it ain't what we're fighting for
so reach out into the falling rain, babe
imagine there is heaven everywhere
ain't no curtain, no backstage, babe
so break a leg, my darling, be square

you went for a walk
without me
thinking I would not
want to go
that I would not
hold your hand
that you would be back before
I could talk you out of it
because you just
wanted to go for a walk
besides
you don't even
have your shoes on
you said

I wrote a book about
a boy flying a kite
it will never sell
you said
no one cares about a boy flying a kite
no one who has ever flown
a kite reads books
you said
sometimes though
they read poems
I said
standing in my bare feet

Index of First lines

a bird in the hand	40
a bowl of buttons	20
ain't no use in howling	73
at the edge of town	34
birds flying to the sound	72
delicate balance	56
dictating parks	7
dyslexic vegan	70
each breath I take expels	60
from monkey to monk	26
frost on pumpkins	8
give me your eyes	47
got clowns in the kitchen	12
grandmother passed away	64
great minds	16
have a nice day	4
I am a fool stumbling	53
I am not as immortal	46
I did not see death	39
I didn't become	18
I do not intend	69
I kiss your roses	57
I saw god the other day	55
I say his death was no accident	10
I wish I could provide you	25

if the pen is mightier	1
it is logical	31
it's been a long time	66
laughter's tears travel	41
leaning against sunset	30
like a drizzling rain	11
lovabetical	27
love is for lovers	45
love is not an asking	9
love makes us equal	33
maybe it weren't no apple	48
no need to manage leftovers	59
now that I've cried	22
one day when nothing else	36
one hand clasping her mirror	68
Picasso Dali & Klee	17
raindrops do not fall	2
Sarah wants a goodnight kiss	51
seldom do scarecrows	23
she wearing apple	50
so many broken dreams	42
so what if paradigms do	54
some silences are louder	65
sometimes I imagine trees	15
starlight evaporates	38

stay in the moment	6
Tex echo station	28
the cost of free will	61
the incidence of birth	24
the narrow burden	3
the shuffling ends	63
they say there is a devil	35
thirsting for simple moisture	19
truth is a door	52
unday blue ribbons	58
unshaken by sizemologists'	37
used to be a day	14
we are a good country	71
we can be all there is	29
we made love beneath the flag	67
"What is love?"	32
while counting the dangers	5
while mr & mrs god	21
will you be sleeping	44
without milk who can be	49
yes your underwear	13
you called the police	43
you went for a walk	74
you worm my heart	62

www.ingramcontent.com/pod-product-compliance
Lightning Source LLC
Chambersburg PA
CBHW051711040426
42446CB00008B/824